Increase your salary now!

MINORITY NEGOTIATIONS

HOW TO MAKE A D.E.A.L
BREAKING GLASS CEILINGS

BY LOREN BASS

Table of Contents

Dedication —————————————— 1

Definition ——————————————— 2

Introduction ——————————————— 3

Chapter 1: Completing a Self-Assessment —— 4

Chapter 2: Personal Branding ——————— 10

Chapter 3: The Importance of Negotiation —— 16

Chapter 4: Make a D.E.A.L ———————— 22

Chapter 5: The Counteroffer ———————— 28

Dedication

A Special Thank You

This book is dedicated to my friends and family who have encouraged me to be great, allowed me to explore and chase my happiness, listened to my random facts and information, and believed in me.

Dream Big

What is a Salary?
Definition

"A salary is part of a compensation package that employers provide to employees in exchange for performing specified services. Generally understood as covering one year's worth of services, it's the money an employee earns at regular intervals — often monthly, semi-monthly or even weekly — throughout the year."- Malcolm Tatum

"A salary employee or salaried employee is paid a fixed amount of money each month. Their earnings are typically supplemented with paid vacations and public holidays, healthcare insurance in country's without universal coverage, and other benefits."- MarketBusinessNews.com

Minority Negotiations

We were never taught the art, until now...

The famous quote by professional ice hockey player Wayne Gretzky goes like this:

"You miss 100% of the shots you don't take."

We hear it in sports, but we don't practice it in the workplace. As a minority, you may fear:

- **How much is too much?** If I go too high will they retract the offer? Will I end up looking greedy?
- **Will I be setting myself up for failure?** A high starting salary may create unrealistically high expectations.
- **What if I need more time off?** What happens if I want to accept the job, but I cannot start by the anticipated start date?

CHAPTER ONE

Completing a Self-Assessment

What do employers want to know?
Take inventory of your strengths

Are you aware of the soft skills and technical skills that employers are looking for? As you progress in an interview the hiring committee or manager will be looking to see if you will be a good fit for their organization.

Step one was getting the interview. Congratulations, your resume passed the test. Now is the time to exhibit your eloquent communication skills in terms of your value that you will bring to this new opportunity. Below are a few examples of skills that employers find valuable.

- **Soft skills:** Communication written and verbal; flexibility; ability to pick up new skills; problem solving
- **Technical skills:** Software proficiency; project management; data analysis
- **FIT:** Work ethic; persistence; ability to work in harmony with the team

How to prove your "value"

Value refers to what you bring to the new role.

From an employer's perspective, each employee has to either (1) increase revenue, or (2) increase margin (ideally both). If you can show to your future employer during the interview process how you can bring additional 'value' to the company (in the form of increased revenue and/or increased margin), you can make a compelling case during your counteroffer.

For example, if you can explain that a new initiative you implemented at your current or previous company saved the company $100,000 by enhancing productivity after reevaluating old project management recommendations, you have now increased your negotiating opportunities. Valuable information such as this makes asking for a $5,000 increase above the initial offer sound a lot more palatable to your future employer.

> *If you don't go after what you want, you'll never have it. If you don't ask, the answer is always no. If you don't step forward, you're always in the same place.* — **Nora Roberts**

Pride versus Humility

Toot your own horn.

"What do you bring to the table? We hear it in terms of relationships, now it is time to understand how to express your skills and talents in the workplace.

Value

CHAPTER TWO

Personal Branding

What is your brand?
More than an employee who executes "job duties"

A manager once told his employees, "If no one else in the company actually knows about your work accomplishments, those accomplishments won't really count for much."

What makes you special above or in comparison to your peers or others?

- **Authentic:** Being genuine about your skills and accomplishments is important as well as showing results.
- **Relevant:** Show how your talents are closely connected to the work being done in that company or department.
- **Unique:** No matter how many people can do the work it's up to you to understand how you execute tasks unlike anyone else. Creativity, efficiency, exceptional public speaking skills- what sets you apart?

Tell your story

By discussing your transferrable skills and/or accomplishments to show the hiring committee or manager what makes you a good fit for the position you will increase your chances to make a counteroffer that will be accepted.

During an offer negotiation, I went from making $35,500 to over $47,000, within two months by discussing my accomplishments in previous roles. Being in the education industry, I emphasized how I helped previous students and departments understand their goals and map out S.M.A.R.T Goals to obtain them.

Understanding your accomplishments, rather than job duties, is important because it will set the tone for what you are bringing to the new organization. You should be able to list at least three (3) accomplishments in your work history that will help you excel in this new role.

- **Job duties** are tasks or expectations that you perform in general. Duties are virtually the same for any employee in a similar role.
- An *accomplishment* is work that is both measurable and unique to the work you completed.

You won't become known and respected in your company if you don't know the unique value you provide and how to connect that value to your company's overall mission.

Did you know that 85 percent of hiring managers report that a candidate's personal brand effects their hiring decisions?

Your personal brand is a reflection of your professional reputation. It should focus on your strengths and communicate the unique elements that you bring to the role. You can exhibit your brand during the interview by how you dress, story telling (expressing your work history using detailed examples), as well as how you effectively engage with the committee or hiring manager. Your personal brand will indicate to employers whether you'll be the right fit for the position.

> **"** Your brand is what people say about you when you are not in the room. **Jeff Bezos "**

How do you answer this:

What do you do?

Eliminate the idea that "my work speaks for itself." Your personal brand will explain how your hard work produces quality and impact in your career; it's not obvious until you make it obvious.

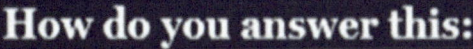

Expertise

CHAPTER THREE

The Importance of Negotiation

Negotiation Opportunities
More than just a number

You've gone through the exhausting process of creating a strong resume that emphasizes your strengths, applying to several jobs that will advance your career, taking multiple interviews, to finally be offered the position you were seeking.

However, the salary you were offered is less than what you desire. Do you turn down this position since it's what you want, or do you ask for a more competitive salary? If you're reading this, my guess is you selected the latter.

Put your fears to the side. You must remember that the employer wants you to be part of their team and many hiring managers will even respect you more for your initiative and negotiation skills.

According to the Job Seeker National Study:
- only 29% of job seekers negotiated their salary
- men are significantly more likely to negotiate their salary versus women
- of all job seekers who attempted to negotiate a higher salary, 84% were successful

Initiating the Negotiation

Let's begin with the key phrase, "Do you mind if I take a couple of days to consider your offer?" Even if a job offer exceeds your expectations, you are still encouraged to negotiate.

This little phrase accomplishes several things- it buys you time to consider the offer, determine the appropriate counteroffer, and begin building your case to support your counteroffer.

Your salary negotiation will be more successful if you carefully choose your counteroffer amount and clearly articulate why you're worth it.

If you are not negotiating the salary, because it suits your needs, be very specific in the other areas of the package you want to negotiate.

For example: there is a pre-planned vacation on your calendar, and you want to make sure you will be able to have the time off, aware that you will not have accrued enough PTO. This is the time to ask for that time off in advanced.

Maybe you believe in professional development and want to make sure you receive it annually. It is important to be clear that your request is for annual professional development at a conference or external opportunity. Be mindful that a webinar could count as professional development, but that may not meet your needs.

Remember: Negotiations are for more than just a salary.

You can ask for (to name a few):

Ask for a different start date or time off, if you had a prior engagement already planned.

Professional development or support funds

Flexible work schedule

Work essentials such as a laptop or work phone, if the job requires remote work responsibilities

> *Everything is negotiable. Whether or not the negotiation is easy is another thing.*
>
> **Carrie Fisher**

Employers worry too!

Prepare to ask.

Here is what hiring managers are thinking when an offer has been made:

"I hope we can pay this person enough."
"I'm afraid that this candidate has multiple offers on the table."
"I really hope this works out."

Confidence

CHAPTER FOUR

Make a D.E.A.L

What is a D.E.A.L?
Understanding how to create a counteroffer

A deal is a mutually beneficial agreement between two or more parties. Key word, mutual! Let me walk you through how I made a good D.E.A.L during a minority salary negotiation.

- **D:** Determine if the first offer is adequate
- **E:** Estimate the cost of living in the area
- **A:** Ascertain average salary for the role
- **L:** Lowest salary you are willing to accept

The Value of a D.E.A.L

Interview- Check
Offer- Check
Accept- not quite yet!

It's time to make a DEAL and not simply accept the first offer made. A job offer is not a gift, make it worth your while! Walk through the D.E.A.L method with me:

After a great interview, I was excited to get the offer, but it was only $42,000, so I **asked to take some time to consider my options**. A jump to $42,000 was more than I was making, but I had promised myself that my next move needed to be my best move and **I wanted no less that an $10,000 increase**.

I took some time to research my industry and noticed that the **average salary** for the role was $42,000, so I was happy that they were not low balling me, but my experience exceeded what the job description listed so I still planned to ask for more.

The **median income** for the area was a little less than $39,000, which made me comfortable as well. Taking into consideration a proposed overtime bill by President Obama, I countered their initial offer of $42,000 with my offer of $47,476 and asked to attend an annual national conference.

I asked for what I felt comfortable with at the time of the job offer because I know it would be hard to come back to the table after the agreements had already been made.

Negotiating can be scary; you should feel comfortable discussing your wants and goals with a trusted advisor. Missed opportunities to negotiate can result in dissatisfaction later.

The wage disparity continues when we undertake this journey alone. Several opportunities exist:

- Speak with a career coach
- Take time to evaluate all benefits (retirement matching, parental leave, sick/paid-time-off, relocation reimbursement, tuition assistance, and more)
- If no salary was posted on the job description reach out to Human Resources and ask for the salary range

> *The most difficult thing in any negotiation, almost, is making sure that you strip it of the emotion and deal with the facts.* **Howard Baker**

Always Make A
D.E.A.L

- Determine if the first offer is adequate
- Estimate the cost-of-living in the area
- Ascertain average salary for the role
- Lowest salary you are willing to accept

ASK

CHAPTER FIVE

The Counteroffer

Words and Phrases to Use

Preparation Time

The following words and phrases are expert-level ways to demonstrate the confidence and knowledge necessary to secure a higher salary.

- **"Based on my research…"**: Rather than just throwing out a number that you think sounds nice, you need to do your homework on what your skills are worth in order to provide a compelling case for an employer to compensate you accordingly.
- **"Market analysis shows…"**: Market refers to what the employee can earn within the industry for similar positions.
- **"If you can do that, I'm on board."**: If you can specifically spell out what it would take for you to accept an offer, you'll be creating clear expectation of your needs.

Understanding the starting point

You should conduct a salary survey that is available from many sources including
- Glassdoor
- Salary.com
- PayScale
- Career One Stop

This will give you a comprehensive overview of the salary ranges for your position in your location. Once you have completed proper research and have evaluated the total compensation packet offered, it's time to make a counteroffer with confidence.

A counteroffer can take place via email or phone call. Be prepared to have a second offer, incase you first counteroffer is not accepted. Do not get defeated, this is natural and a part of the process. You may not need the second offer, but start high at your primary want, then be comfortable with your second offer if the first offer is not accepted.

The ultimate part of negotiating is understanding what will make you walk away from an opportunity or agreeing to terms that make you happy. Finally, get the final agreement in writing to acknowledge the DEAL is closed.

Every offer will not be in your best interest. Companies will attempt to offer you the lowest they think you will accept. It's up to you to turn the cards in your favor; no one owes you anything.

Sometimes an offer is firm due to budget allocation and restraints, this is why total compensation is important to review. If you focus only on the salary you could be missing out.

> *Let us never negotiate out of fear. But let us never fear to negotiate.*
>
> John F. Kennedy

Note:

Remember...

"Never engage in negotiation as an ultimatum — an either/or — but rather as a collaborative process and a unique opportunity to create a compensation package that makes sense for both you and for them. Establish priorities as to what is most important to you and what items you are willing to trade off." Roy Cohen

You got this!

About the Author
Meet Loren Bass

Loren Bass is the CEO/President of Bass Empire LLC, a Center of Innovation distinguished in creating specialty products, aiding in career development, as well as assisting small businesses in launching from idea to inception. She holds a Bachelor of Fine Arts and a Master of Education from Valdosta State University where she serves as an African American Studies Professor.

Loren's passion for helping others is fueled from her background in speech communications, negotiations, and developing leaders.

Her hunger for knowledge and go-getter determination to turn information into action has awarded her opportunities to present at the NASPA, Student Affairs Administrators in Higher Education, 2019 national conference in Los Angeles, as well as being featured as a 2020 TedX speaker at Valdosta State University. Both presentations focused on opportunities to negotiate when the stakes are high.

To connect with Loren:
Email: llbass@valdosta.edu
Facebook: BassConsulting
Follow on Instagram: Bass_Consulting

www.ingramcontent.com/pod-product-compliance
Lightning Source LLC
Chambersburg PA
CBHW041943240526
45473CB00033B/499